Shell Scripting

JASON CANNON

JASON CANNON

Contents

JASON CANNON

OTHER BOOKS BY THE AUTHOR

Command Line Kung Fu: Bash Scripting Tricks, Linux Shell Programming
Tips, and Bash One-liners
http://www.linuxtrainingacademy.com/command-line-kung-fu-book

High Availability for the LAMP Stack: Eliminate Single Points of Failure
and Increase Uptime for Your Linux, Apache, MySQL, and PHP Based
Web Applications
http://www.linuxtrainingacademy.com/ha-lamp-book

Linux for Beginners: An Introduction to the Linux Operating System and
Command Line
http://www.linuxtrainingacademy.com/linux

Python Programming for Beginners
http://www.linuxtrainingacademy.com/python-programming-for-
beginners

INTRODUCTION

I'm lazy. I admit it. I believe so strongly in being lazy that I'll do almost anything to facilitate even more laziness in the future.

For example, if I think there is a slight chance that I will ever have to perform the same set of commands again, I create a shell script then and there. When I need to do that task again, I lazily execute my script. If maintenance needs to be performed on a system at 2:00 in the morning, I write a script that does the required work and schedule a job to run it. Lazy people love to sleep.

I also believe in helping people find their inner laziness. Why? Because lazy people solve problems. They eliminate the unnecessary. They simplify the complex.

That's the reason I've written this book.

I want to share with you some of my favorite tips and tricks I've used to automate repetitive, monotonous, tedious, and complex tasks. May they inspire you to be lazy.

Before we get started I recommend that you download the shell scripts used in this book by visiting:
http://www.linuxtrainingacademy.com/shell-scripts

SHELL SCRIPTING, SUCCINCTLY

A script is a command line program that contains a series of commands. The commands contained in the script are executed by an interpreter. In the case of shell scripts, the shell acts as the interpreter and executes the commands listed in the script one after the other.

Anything you can execute at the command line, you can put into a shell script. Shell scripts are great at automating tasks. If you find yourself running a series of commands to accomplish a given task and will need to perform that task again in the future, you can—and probably should—create a shell script for that task.

Let's look at a simple shell script. The name of this script is **script1.sh**.

```
#!/bin/bash
echo "Scripting is fun!"
```

Before you try to execute the script, make sure that it is executable.

```
$ chmod 755 script1.sh
```

Here is what happens when you execute the script.

```
$ ./script1.sh
Scripting is fun!
$
```

The Shebang

You'll notice that the first line of the script starts with **#!** followed by the path to the bash shell program, **/bin/bash**. The number sign is very similar to the sharp sign used in music notation. Also, some people refer to the exclamation mark as a "bang." So, **#!** can be spoken as "sharp bang." The term "Shebang" is an inexact contraction of "sharp bang."

When a script's first line starts with a shebang, what follows is used as the interpreter for the commands listed in the script. Here are three examples of shell scripts, each using a different shell program as the interpreter.

```
#!/bin/csh
echo "This script uses csh as the interpreter."
```

```
#!/bin/ksh
echo "This script uses ksh as the interpreter."
```

```
#!/bin/zsh
echo "This script uses zsh as the interpreter."
```

When you execute a script that contains a shebang, what actually happens is that the interpreter is executed and the path used to call the script is passed as an argument to the interpreter. You can prove this by examining the process table.

Let's start this script, **sleepy.sh**, in the background and look at the process table.

The contents of **sleepy.sh**:

```
#!/bin/bash
```

```
sleep 90
```

Let's execute it in the background and take a look at the processes.

```
$ ./sleepy.sh &
[1] 16796
$ ps -fp 16796
UID         PID  PPID  C STIME TTY          TIME CMD
jason     16796 16725  0 22:50 pts/0    00:00:00
/bin/bash ./sleepy.sh
$
```

You can see that what is actually running is **/bin/bash ./sleepy.sh**. Let's use a full path to the script.

```
$ /tmp/sleepy.sh &
[1] 16804
$ ps -fp 16804
UID         PID  PPID  C STIME TTY          TIME CMD
jason     16804 16725  0 22:51 pts/0    00:00:00
/bin/bash /tmp/sleepy.sh
$
```

Sure enough, **/bin/bash /tmp/sleepy.sh** is being executed. Also, you can see that **/bin/bash** is executing the sleep command, which is the first and only command command in the shell script.

```
$ ps -ef| grep 16804 | grep -v grep
jason     16804 16725  0 22:51 pts/0    00:00:00
/bin/bash /tmp/sleepy.sh
jason     16805 16804  0 22:51 pts/0    00:00:00
sleep 90
$ pstree -p 16804
sleepy.sh(16804)——sleep(16805)
$
```

If you do not supply a shebang and specify an interpreter on the first line of the script, the commands in the script will be executed using your current shell. Even though this can work just fine under many circumstances, it's best to be explicit and specify the exact interpreter to be used with the script. For example, there are features and syntax that work just fine with the bash shell that will not work with the csh shell.

Also, you don't have to use a shell as the interpreter for your scripts. Here is an example of a Python script named **hi.py**.

```
#!/usr/bin/python
print "This is a Python script."
```

Let's make it executable and run it.

```
$ chmod 755 hi.py
$ ./hi.py
This is a Python script.
$
```

For more information on python programming and scripting, see my book *Python Programming for Beginners* at http://www.linuxtrainingacademy.com/python-book.

Let's get back to shell scripting.

Variables

You can use variables in your shell scripts. Variables are simply storage locations that have a name. You can think of variables as name-value pairs. To assign a value to a variable, use the syntax **VARIABLE_NAME="Value"**. Do not use spaces before or after the equals sign. Also, variables are case sensitive, and, by convention, variable names are in uppercase.

```
#!/bin/bash
MY_SHELL="bash"
```

To use a variable, precede the variable name with a dollar sign.

```
#!/bin/bash
MY_SHELL="bash"
echo "I like the $MY_SHELL shell."
```

You can also enclose the variable name in curly braces and precede the opening brace with a dollar sign. Syntax: **${VARIABLE_NAME}**.

```
#!/bin/bash
MY_SHELL="bash"
echo "I like the ${MY_SHELL} shell."
```

Here is the output of the script:

```
I like the bash shell.
```

The curly brace syntax is optional unless you need to immediately precede or follow the variable with additional data.

```
#!/bin/bash
MY_SHELL="bash"
echo "I am ${MY_SHELL}ing on my keyboard."
```

Output:

```
I am bashing on my keyboard.
```

If you do not encapsulate the variable name in curly braces the shell will treat the additional text as part of the variable name. Since a variable with that name does not exist, nothing is put in its place.

```
#!/bin/bash
MY_SHELL="bash"
echo "I am $MY_SHELLing on my keyboard."
```

Output:

```
I am  on my keyboard.
```

You can also assign the output of a command to a variable. To do this, enclose the command in parentheses and precede it with a dollar sign.

```
#!/bin/bash
SERVER_NAME=$(hostname)
echo "You are running this script on ${SERVER_NAME}."
```

The output of the command **hostname** is stored in the variable **SERVER_NAME**. In this sample output, the server name is **linuxsvr**.

```
You are running this script on linuxsvr.
```

You can also enclose the command in back ticks. This is an older syntax being replaced by the **$()** syntax. However, you may see this in older scripts.

```
#!/bin/bash
SERVER_NAME=`hostname`
echo "You are running this script on ${SERVER_NAME}."
```

Valid Variable Names

Variable names can contain letters, digits, and underscores. They can start with letters or underscores, but cannot start with a digit. Here are examples of valid variable names.

```
FIRST3LETTERS="ABC"
FIRST_THREE_LETTERS="ABC"
firstThreeLetters="ABC"
```

Here are some examples of invalid variable names.

```
3LETTERS="ABC"
first-three-letters="ABC"
first@Three@Letters="ABC"
```

Tests

Scripts are designed to replace the need for a person to physically be at a keyboard and type in a series of commands. What if you have a task you want to automate, but it requires different actions based on different circumstances? Since a person may not be around to make decisions when the script needs to run, we'll need to test for those conditions and have the script act accordingly.

To create a test, place a conditional expression between brackets. The syntax is: **[condition-to-test-for]**. You can test for several types of situations. For example, you can compare if strings are equal, if a number is greater than another one, or if a file exists. This test checks to see if **/etc/passwd** exists. If it does, it returns true. I.e., the command exits with a status of 0. If the file doesn't exist it returns false. I.e., the command exits with a status of 1.

```
[ -e /etc/passwd ]
```

If you are using the bash shell, you can run the command **help test** to see the various types of tests you can perform. You can also read the man page for test: **man test**. Here are of some of the more common tests you can perform.

```
File operators:
  -d FILE        True if file is a directory.
  -e FILE        True if file exists.
  -f FILE        True if file exists and is a regular
file.
  -r FILE        True if file is readable by you.
  -s FILE        True if file exists and is not
empty.
  -w FILE        True if the file is writable by you.
  -x FILE        True if the file is executable by
you.

String operators:
  -z STRING      True if string is empty.
  -n STRING      True if string is not empty.
     STRING      True if string is not empty.
  STRING1 = STRING2
                 True if the strings are equal.
  STRING1 != STRING2
                 True if the strings are not equal.
Arithmetic operators:
  arg1 -eq arg2  True if arg1 is equal to arg2.
  arg1 -ne arg2  True if arg1 is not equal to arg2.
  arg1 -lt arg2  True if arg1 is less than arg2.
  arg1 -le arg2  True if arg1 is less than or equal
to  arg2.
  arg1 -gt arg2  True if arg1 is greater than arg2.
  arg1 -ge arg2  True if arg1 is greater than or
equal to arg2.
```

The if Statement

Now that you know how to determine if a certain condition is true or not, you can combine that with the **if** statement to make decisions in your scripts.

The **if** statement starts with the word "**if**" and is then followed by a test. The following line contains the word **then**. Next comes a series of commands that will be executed if the tested condition is true. Finally, the **if** statement ends with **fi**, which is **if** spelled backwards. Here is the syntax.

```
if [ condition-true ]
then
    command 1
    command 2
    . . .
fi
```

Here is an example:

```
#!/bin/bash
MY_SHELL="bash"

if [ "$MY_SHELL" = "bash" ]
then
    echo "You seem to like the bash shell."
fi
```

It is a best practice to enclose variables in quotes to prevent some unexpected side effects when performing conditional tests. Here is the output of running the script:

```
You seem to like the bash shell.
```

You can also perform an action if the condition is not true by using an **if/else** statement. Here is what an **if/else** statement looks like.

```
if [ condition-true ]
then
    command 1
```

```
   command 2
   . . .
else  #
   command 3
   command 4
   . . .
fi
```

Let's update the script to perform an action if the statement is not true.

```
#!/bin/bash
MY_SHELL="csh"

if [ "$MY_SHELL" = "bash" ]
then
   echo "You seem to like the bash shell."
else
   echo "You don't seem to like the bash shell."
fi
```

Here is the output. Because **["$MY_SHELL" = "bash"]** evaluated to false the statements following **else** were executed.

```
You don't seem to like the bash shell.
```

You can also test for multiple conditions using the **elif**. The word **elif** is a contraction for "else if." Like **If**, follow **elif** with a condition to test for. On the following line, use the word **then**. Finally, provide a series of commands to execute if the condition evaluates as true.

```
if [ condition-true ]
then
   command 1
   command 2
   . . .
elif [ condition-true ]
then
   command 3
   command 4
   . . .
else  #
   command 5
```

```
    command 6
    ...
fi
```

Here is an updated script using **elif**.

```
#!/bin/bash
MY_SHELL="csh"

if [ "$MY_SHELL" = "bash" ]
then
    echo "You seem to like the bash shell."
elif [ "$MY_SHELL" = "csh" ]
then
  echo "You seem to like the csh shell."
else
  echo "You don't seem to like the bash or csh
shells."
fi
```

Output:

```
You seem to like the csh shell.
```

The for Loop

If you want to perform an action on a list of items, use a **for** loop. The first line of a **for** loop start with the word "**for**" followed by a variable name, followed by the word "**in**" and then a list of items. The next line contains the word "**do**". Place the statements you want to execute on the following lines and, finally, end the **for** loop with the word "**done**" on a single line.

```
for VARIABLE_NAME in ITEM_1 ITEM_2 ITEM_N
do
  command 1
  command 2
  ...
done
```

Essentially what happens is that the first item in the list is assigned to the variable and the code block is executed. The next item in the list is then assigned to the variable and the commands are executed. This happens for each item in the list.

Here is a simple script that shows how a **for** loop works.

```
#!/bin/bash
for COLOR in red green blue
do
  echo "COLOR: $COLOR"
done
```

Output:

```
COLOR: red
COLOR: green
COLOR: blue
```

It's a common practice for the list of items to be stored in a variable as in this example.

```
#!/bin/bash
COLORS="red green blue"

for COLOR in $COLORS
do
  echo "COLOR: $COLOR"
done
```

Output:

```
COLOR: red
COLOR: green
COLOR: blue
```

This shell script, **rename-pics.sh**, renames all of the files that end in **jpg** by prepending today's date to the original file name.

```
#!/bin/bash
PICTURES=$(ls *jpg)
DATE=$(date +%F)
```

```
for PICTURE in $PICTURES
do
   echo "Renaming ${PICTURE} to ${DATE}-${PICTURE}"
   mv ${PICTURE} ${DATE}-${PICTURE}
done
```

Here's what happens when you run this script.

```
$ ls
bear.jpg  man.jpg  pig.jpg  rename-pics.sh
$ ./rename-pics.sh
Renaming bear.jpg to 2015-03-06-bear.jpg
Renaming man.jpg to 2015-03-06-man.jpg
Renaming pig.jpg to 2015-03-06-pig.jpg
$ ls
2015-03-06-bear.jpg  2015-03-06-man.jpg  2015-03-06-
pig.jpg  rename-pics.sh
$
```

Positional Parameters

Positional parameters are variables that contain the contents of the command line. These variables are $0 through $9. The script itself is stored in $0, the first parameter in $1, the second in $2, and so on. Take this command line as an example.

```
$ script.sh parameter1 parameter2 parameter3
```

The contents are as follows: $0 is "script.sh", $1 is "parameter1", $2 is "parameter2", and $3 is "parameter3".

This script, **archive_user.sh**, accepts a parameter which is a username.

```
#!/bin/bash

echo "Executing script: $0"
echo "Archiving user: $1"

# Lock the account
passwd -l $1
```

```
# Create an archive of the home directory.
tar cf /archives/${1}.tar.gz /home/${1}
```

Comments

Anything that follows the pound sign is a comment. The only exception to this is the shebang on the first line. Everywhere else in the script where a pound sign is encountered marks the beginning of a comment. Comments are dutifully ignored by the interpreter as they are for the benefit of us humans.

Anything that follows the pound sign is ignored. If a pound sign starts at the beginning of a line, the entire line is ignored. If a pound sign is encountered in the middle of a line, only the information to the right of the pound sign is ignored.

Here is what the output looks like when we execute the **archive_user.sh** script.

```
$ ./archive_user.sh elvis
Executing script: ./archive_user.sh
Archiving user: elvis
passwd: password expiry information changed.
tar: Removing leading `/' from member names
$
```

Instead of referring to $1 throughout the script, let's assign its value to a more meaningful variable name.

```
#!/bin/bash

USER=$1    # The first parameter is the user.

echo "Executing script: $0"
echo "Archiving user: $USER"

# Lock the account
passwd -l $USER
```

```
# Create an archive of the home directory.
tar cf /archives/${USER}.tar.gz /home/${USER}
```

The output remains the same.

```
$ ./archive_user.sh elvis
Executing script: ./archive_user.sh
Archiving user: elvis
passwd: password expiry information changed.
tar: Removing leading `/' from member names
$
```

You can access all the positional parameters starting at $1 to the very last one on the command line by using the special variable **$@**. Here is how to update the **archive_user.sh** script to accept one or more parameters.

```
#!/bin/bash

echo "Executing script: $0"

for USER in $@
do
  echo "Archiving user: $USER"

  # Lock the account
  passwd -l $USER

  # Create an archive of the home directory.
  tar cf /archives/${USER}.tar.gz /home/${USER}
done
```

Let's pass in multiple users to the script.

```
$ ./archive_user.sh chet joe
Executing script: ./archive_user.sh
Archiving user: chet
passwd: password expiry information changed.
tar: Removing leading `/' from member names
Archiving user: joe
passwd: password expiry information changed.
tar: Removing leading `/' from member names
```

Getting User Input

If you want to accept standard input, use the **read** command. Remember that standard input typically comes from a person typing at the keyboard, but it can also come from other sources, like the output of a command in a command pipeline. The format for the **read** command is **read -p "PROMPT" VARIABLE_NAME**. This version of the archive_user.sh script asks for the user account.

```
#!/bin/bash

read -p "Enter a user name: " USER

echo "Archiving user: $USER"

# Lock the account
passwd -l $USER

# Create an archive of the home directory.
tar cf /archives/${USER}.tar.gz /home/${USER}
```

Let's run this script and archive the **mitch** account.

```
$ ./archive_user.sh
Enter a user name: mitch
Archiving user: mitch
passwd: password expiry information changed.
tar: Removing leading `/' from member names
$
```

Review

The first line in a shell script should start with a shebang and the path to the interpreter that should be used to execute the script.

To assign a value to a variable, start with the variable name followed by an equals sign followed by the value. Do not use a space before or after the equals sign.

You can access the value stored in a variable by using **$VARIABLE_NAME** or **${VARIABLE_NAME}**. The latter form is required if you want to precede or follow the variable with additional data.

To assign the output of a command to a variable, enclose the command in parentheses and precede it with a dollar sign. **VARIABLE_NAME=$(command)**

Perform tests by placing an expression in brackets. Tests are typically combined with **if** statements.

Use **if**, **if/else**, or **if/elif/else** statements to make decisions in your scripts.

To perform an action or series of action on multiple items, use a **for** loop.

To access items on the command line, use positions parameters. The name of the program is represented by **$0**, the first parameter is represented by **$1**, and so on. To access all the items on the command line starting at the first parameter (**$1**), use the special variable **$@**.

You can place comments in your scripts by using the pound sign.

Accept user input by using the **read** command.

Practice Exercises

Exercise 1:

Write a shell script that prints "Shell Scripting is Fun!" on the screen.

Hint 1: Remember to make the shell script executable with the chmod command.

Hint 2: Remember to start your script with a shebang!

Exercise 2:

Modify the shell script from exercise 1 to include a variable. The variable will hold the contents of the message "Shell Scripting is Fun!".

Exercise 3:

Store the output of the command "hostname" in a variable. Display "This script is running on _____." where "_____" is the output of the "hostname" command.

Hint: It's a best practice to use the **${VARIABLE}** syntax if there is text or characters that directly precede or follow the variable.

Exercise 4:

Write a shell script to check to see if the file "/etc/shadow" exists. If it does exist, display "Shadow passwords are enabled." Next, check to see if you can write to the file. If you can, display "You have permissions to edit /etc/shadow." If you cannot, display "You do NOT have permissions to edit /etc/shadow."

Exercise 5:

Write a shell script that displays "man", "bear", "pig", "dog", "cat", and "sheep" on the screen with each appearing on a separate line. Try to do this in as few lines as possible.

Hint: Loops can be used to perform repetitive tasks.

Exercise 6:

Write a shell script that prompts the user for a name of a file or directory and reports if it is a regular file, a directory, or another type of file.

Also perform an **ls** command against the file or directory with the long listing option.

Exercise 7:

Modify the previous script so that it accepts the file or directory name as an argument instead of prompting the user to enter it.

Exercise 8:

Modify the previous script to accept an unlimited number of files and directories as arguments.

Hint: You'll want to use a special variable.

Solutions to the Practice Exercises

Exercise 1:

```
#!/bin/bash
echo "Shell Scripting is Fun!"
```

Exercise 2:

```
#!/bin/bash
MESSAGE="Shell Scripting is Fun!"
echo "$MESSAGE"
```

Exercise 3:

```
#!/bin/bash
HOST_NAME=$(hostname)
echo "This script is running on ${HOST_NAME}."
```

Exercise 4:

```
#!/bin/bash

FILE="/etc/shadow"

if [ -e "$FILE" ]
then
  echo "Shadow passwords are enabled."
fi
```

```
if [ -w "$FILE" ]
then
  echo "You have permissions to edit ${FILE}."
else
  echo "You do NOT have permissions to edit ${FILE}."
fi
```

Exercise 5:

```
#!/bin/bash
for ANIMAL in man bear pig dog cat sheep
do
  echo "$ANIMAL"
done
```

Exercise 6:

```
#!/bin/bash

read -p "Enter the path to a file or a directory: "
FILE

if [ -f "$FILE" ]
then
  echo "$FILE is a regular file."
elif [ -d "$FILE" ]
then
  echo "$FILE is a directory."
else
  echo "$FILE is something other than a regular file
or directory."
fi

ls -l $FILE
```

Exercise 7:

```
#!/bin/bash

FILE=$1

if [ -f "$FILE" ]
```

```
then
  echo "$FILE is a regular file."
elif [ -d "$FILE" ]
then
  echo "$FILE is a directory."
else
  echo "$FILE is something other than a regular file
or directory."
fi

ls -l $FILE
```

Exercise 8:

```
#!/bin/bash

for FILE in $@
do
  if [ -f "$FILE" ]
  then
    echo "$FILE is a regular file."
  elif [ -d "$FILE" ]
  then
    echo "$FILE is a directory."
  else
    echo "$FILE is something other than a regular
file or directory."
  fi

  ls -l $FILE
done
```

EXIT STATUSES AND RETURN CODES

In this chapter, you will learn how to determine the exit status of a given command. You'll learn how to make decisions in your scripts based on the exit statuses of various commands. Finally, you'll learn how to use exit statuses in your own scripts.

Every time a command is executed it returns an exit status. The exit status, which is sometimes called a return code or exit code, is an integer ranging from 0 to 255. By convention, commands that execute successfully return a 0 exit status. If some sort of error is encountered, then a non-zero exit status is returned.

These return codes can be used in your script for error checking. It can be a simple test, like checking for a zero return code, or it could be more complex, like checking for a specific error code.

If you want to find out what the various exit statuses mean, you have to consult the documentation for the given command or look at its source code. You can use the **man** and **info** commands to read the documentation for most commands on your system. For example, in the **grep** man page, it explains **grep** will exit with a status of 0 if the search pattern is found and 1 if it is not.

The special variable **$?** contains the return code of the previously executed command. In this shell script snippet, the **ls** command is called with a path to a file that doesn't exist.

```
ls /not/here
echo "$?"
```

Output:

```
ls: /not/here: No such file or directory
2
```

Immediately after the **ls** command is executed, the return code of that command is displayed on the screen using **echo $?**. This will display a **2** on the screen. Remember that non-zero exit codes indicate some sort of error. Had the file **/not/here** existed and if **ls** was able to display information about that file successfully, the exit status would have been **0**.

You can use the exit status of a command to make a decision or perform a different action based on the exit status. In this example shell script snippet, we use the ping command to test our network connectivity to www.google.com. The **-c** option for the **ping** command simply tells **ping** to send just one packet.

```
HOST="google.com"
ping -c 1 $HOST
if [ "$?" -eq "0" ]
then
  echo "$HOST reachable."
else
  echo "$HOST unreachable."
fi
```

After the **ping** command is executed, we check the exit status. If the exit status is equal to 0, then we **echo** to the screen that google.com is reachable.

If the exit status is NOT equal to 0 we **echo** to the screen that google.com is unreachable.

This example just checks for an error condition. In the **if** statement, we look for a non-zero exit status. If **$?** does not equal zero, then we **echo** that the host is unreachable. If the **ping** command succeeds and returns a 0 exit status, then the **echo** statement is not executed.

```
HOST="google.com"

ping -c 1 $HOST

if [ "$?" -ne "0" ]
then
  echo "$HOST unreachable."
fi
```

We can assign the return code of a command to variable and then use that variable later in the script. In this example, the value of **$?** is assigned to the **RETURN_CODE** variable. So, **RETURN_CODE** contains the exit status of the **ping** command.

```
HOST="google.com"
ping -c 1 $HOST
RETURN_CODE=$?

if [ "$RETURN_CODE" -ne "0" ]
then
  echo "$HOST unreachable."
fi
```

In addition to using if statements with exit statuses, you can use logical ANDs and ORs. The double ampersand (**&&**) represents AND, while the double pipe (**||**) represents OR. You can chain together multiple commands with either ANDS or ORS.

The command following a double ampersand will only execute if the previous command succeeds. In other words, the command following a double ampersand will only run if the previous command exits with a 0 exit status.

In the following example, **mkdir /tmp/bak** is executed. If it succeeds and returns a 0 exit status, then, and only then, will the **cp** command be executed. In this example, you can see there is no need for the **cp** command to be executed if the directory wasn't able to be created.

```
mkdir /tmp/bak && cp test.txt /tmp/bak/
```

The command following a double pipe will only execute if the previous command fails. If the first command returns a non-zero exit status, then the next command is executed.

In the following example, the first **cp** command, **cp test.txt /tmp/bak/**, is executed. If it succeeds the next **cp** command is NOT executed. In that instance, if the first **cp** command succeeds, we have successfully created a backup copy of **test.txt** so the there is no need for another backup copy of that file. If the first command fails, then the second command is executed. If test.txt can't be copied into **/tmp/bak**, an attempt will be make to copy it to **/tmp**. With an OR, only one of the two commands will successfully execute.

```
cp test.txt /tmp/bak/ || cp test.txt /tmp
```

Let's revisit our earlier example. Instead of using an **if** statement, here we are using an AND. This time, if the ping command exits with a 0 exit status, then "google.com reachable" will be echoed to the screen.

```
#!/bin/bash
HOST="google.com"
ping -c 1 $HOST && echo "$HOST reachable."
```

Here we are using an OR instead of an **if** statement. In this example, If the **ping** command fails, then "google.com unreachable" will be echoed to the screen. If the **ping** command succeeds, the **echo** statement will not be executed.

```
#!/bin/bash
HOST="google.com"
```

JASON CANNON

```
ping -c 1 $HOST || echo "$HOST unreachable."
```

If you want to chain commands together on a single line, you can do that by separating those commands with a semicolon. The semicolon does not perform exit status checking. The command following a semicolon will always get executed, no matter if the previous command failed or succeeded.

Separating commands with a semicolon is the same as putting the command on separate lines. I rarely use semicolons to separate commands in shell scripts, but you might see this in existing shells scripts. Of course, you can also use this syntax on the command line outside of a shell script. The following two examples are identical in function.

```
cp test.txt /tmp/bak/ ; cp test.txt /tmp
```

```
cp test.txt /tmp/bak/
cp test.txt /tmp
```

The `exit` Command

Not only do normal commands return an exit status, but shell scripts do as well. You can control the exit status of your shell script by using the **exit** command. Simply use the **exit** command in your script and follow it with a number from 0 to 255.

If you do not specify a return code with the **exit** command, then the exit status of the previously executed command is used as the exit status. This is also true if you do not include the exit command at all in your shell script. Again, in that case, the last command that was executed in your shell script will determine the return code for your entire shell script.

Also note that you can use the **exit** command anywhere in your shell script. Whenever the exit command is reached, your shell script will stop running.

In this example, we are controlling the exit status of our script with the exit command.

```
#!/bin/bash
HOST="google.com"
ping -c 1 $HOST
if [ "$?" -ne "0" ]
then
    echo "$HOST unreachable."
    exit 1
fi
exit 0
```

If the **ping** command succeeds, a return code of 0 is received. This means that the test in the **if** statement is false and that code block will not execute. That means the **exit 0** line is executed. This stops the execution of the script and returns a 0 exit status.

If the **ping** command fails, then a non-zero exit status is received. That makes the **if** statement true, and the **echo** command and **exit 1** commands are executed. The **exit 1** command will stop the execution of the script and return an exit status of 1. Now your shell script can be called by another shell script and its exit status can be examined just like any other command.

Since you control the exit statuses, you can make them have a significant meaning. Maybe a return code of 1 means that one type of error occurred while a return code of 2 means that a different type of error occurred. If you have scripts that are executing other scripts, then you can program accordingly to these returns codes if you need or want to.

Review

In this chapter, you learned that all commands return an exit status.

Valid exit statuses are numbers that range from 0 to 255, with a zero exit status representing the successful execution of a command and a non-zero status representing an error condition.

You learned about the special variable $? and how it contains the value of the exit status of the previously executed command.

You made decisions using the exit status of command by using **if** statements, ANDs, and ORs.

Finally, you learned how to control the exit statuses of your own shell scripts by using the exit command.

Practice Exercises

Exercise 1:

Write a shell script that displays, "This script will exit with a 0 exit status." Be sure that the script does indeed exit with a 0 exit status.

Exercise 2:

Write a shell script that accepts a file or directory name as an argument. Have the script report if it is a regular file, a directory, or another type of file. If it is a regular file, exit with a 0 exit status. If it is a directory, exit with a 1 exit status. If it is some other type of file, exit with a 2 exit status.

Exercise 3:

Write a script that executes the command "cat /etc/shadow". If the command returns a 0 exit status, report "Command succeeded" and exit with a 0 exit status. If the command returns a non-zero exit status, report "Command failed" and exit with a 1 exit status.

Solutions to the Practice Exercises

Exercise 1:

```
#!/bin/bash

echo "This script will exit with a 0 exit status."
exit 0
```

Exercise 2:

```
#!/bin/bash

echo "This script will exit with a 0 exit status."
exit 0
```

Exercise 3:

```
#!/bin/bash

cat /etc/shadow
if [ "$?" -eq "0" ]
then
  echo "Command succeeded"
  exit 0
else
  echo "Command failed"
  exit 1
fi
```

JASON CANNON

FUNCTIONS

In this chapter, you'll learn why and when you'll want to use functions. You'll learn how to create functions as well as how to use them. We'll talk about variables and their scope. You'll learn how to use parameters to access the arguments passed to your function. Finally, you'll learn how to handle exit statuses and return codes with functions.

There is a concept in computer programming and application development known as DRY. DRY stands for Don't Repeat Yourself. Functions allow you to write a block of code once and use it many times. Instead of repeating several lines of code each time you need to perform a particular task—or function—simply call the function that contains that code. This helps in reducing the length of your scripts and also gives you a single place to change, test, troubleshoot, and document a given task. All of this makes your scripts easier to maintain.

Whenever you need to perform the same action multiple times in a script, that's a sign that you should probably write a function for that action. A function is simply a block of reusable code that performs an action and returns an exit status or return code. A function must be defined before it is called. When you call a function, you can pass data into the function. You can access that data within your function as parameters.

Creating a Function

There are two ways to create a function. The first way is to explicitly use the keyword **function**, then follow it by the function's name, and then a set of parenthesis. Next you'll use an opening curly brace. The code or commands that follow will be executed when the function is called. To end your function, use a closing curly brace.

```
function function-name() {
    # Code goes here.
}
```

The second way to declare a function is exactly like the first except that you do not use the keyword function in your declaration. Everything else stays the same.

```
function-name() {
    # Code goes here.
}
```

Calling a Function

To call the function, simply list its name on a line in the script. When calling the function, do not use parentheses. You may have seen this syntax and style in other programming languages, but it doesn't work in shell scripts. Simply place the name of a function on a line and it will execute that function.

When you run this script, the word "Hello!" is displayed on the screen.

```
#!/bin/bash

function hello() {
    echo "Hello!"
}

hello
```

Be aware that functions can call other functions. In this script, the **hello** function is declared. Next, the **now** function is declared. Finally, the hello function is called. When the **hello** function is called, it prints "Hello!" on the screen and then calls the **now** function, which prints the current time to the screen.

```
#!/bin/bash

function hello() {
    echo "Hello!"
    now
}
function now() {
    echo "It's $(date +%r)"
}

hello
```

You might have caught that the **now** function was defined after the **hello** function. I said that functions had to be declared before they are used and, in this example, that is exactly what has happened. Even though the **hello** function calls the **now** function, and the **now** function is below it in the script, the **now** function actually gets read into the script before the **hello** function is called. So, in the order of execution, it is defined before it is used.

Do not do this:

```
#!/bin/bash
function hello() {
    echo "Hello!"
    now
}
hello
function now() {
    echo "It's $(date +%r)"
}
```

If you were to run that script, it would throw an error stating that **now** wasn't found. This is because **hello** gets executed before the **now** function is declared, or read, into the script.

This is really the main point of scripting languages. They are not pre-compiled. In some languages, you can define a function anywhere and the compiler will examine all of the source code before piecing it all together for the final execution of the program. In a script, the commands and components are read from the top to the bottom at run time.

Note that it's a best practice to place all of your functions at the top of your script. This ensures they are all defined before they are used.

Positional Parameters

Like shell scripts themselves, functions can accept parameters. Also like shell scripts, you can access the values of these passed in parameters using **$1**, **$2**, and so on. You can even access all the parameters passed into the function using **$@**. The only difference is that **$0** is still the name of the script itself. You can't access the name of the function using **$0**, but the good news is that you'll never really want to anyway.

To send data to a function, supply the data after the function name. In this example, the **hello** function is called with one parameter, **Jason**. This means the contents of **$1** inside the hello function are "**Jason**". As you can guess, the output of this script is simply "Hello Jason".

```
#!/bin/bash
function hello() {
    echo "Hello $1"
}
hello Jason
```

Output:

```
Hello Jason
```

This script will loop through each of the parameters passed to the hello function and echo "Hello" followed by the parameter. This output of this script would be three lines. The first line would be "Hello Jason", the second line would be "Hello Dan", and the third line would be "Hello Ryan".

```
#!/bin/bash
function hello() {
    for NAME in $@
    do
        echo "Hello $NAME"
    done
}
hello Jason Dan Ryan
```

Output:

```
Hello Jason
Hello Dan
Hello Ryan
```

Variable Scope

By default, all variables are global. This means that the variable and its value can be accessed anywhere in the script, including in any function. The only small catch is that the variable has to be defined before it can be used. You can't assign a value to a variable at the very end of your script and access that value via the variable at the very top. If you attempt that, the contents of that variable will be blank as it hasn't been given a value yet. This is true for functions as well. If a function uses a global variable, that variable has to be defined before the function is called.

If we look at this snippet of a shell script, you'll see that the variable, **GLOBAL_VAR**, is defined before the function is called. In this case, the value of **GLOBAL_VAR** can be accessed in the function.

```
GLOBAL_VAR=1
# GLOBAL_VAR is available
```

```
# in the function.
my_function
```

Here is an example of the opposite. Since the variable, **GLOBAL_VAR**, is defined after the function is called, it is not available in the function.

```
# GLOBAL_VAR is NOT available
# in the function.
my_function
GLOBAL_VAR=1
```

If a global variable is defined in a function, it is not available outside that function until the function is called and executed. At the top of the next script, the **my_function** function is declared. It hasn't been executed yet. If we attempt to use the variable defined within the function without calling it first, the value of the variable will be empty. In this example, the first **echo** statement will simply print a blank line.

Next, the **my_function** function is called. Now a value has been assigned to the variable named **GLOBAL_VAR**. On the **echo** statement after the function call, it will print "1" because that is the value now assigned to **GLOBAL_VAR**.

```
#!/bin/bash

my_function() {
    GLOBAL_VAR=1
}

# GLOBAL_VAR not available yet.
echo $GLOBAL_VAR

my_function

# GLOBAL_VAR is NOW available.
echo $GLOBAL_VAR
```

Local Variables

A local variable is a variable that can only be accessed within the function in which it is declared. Use the **local** keyword before the variable name. Only use the **local** keyword the first time the local variable is used. Note that the **local** keyword can only be used inside a function.

It's a best practice to use local variables inside of your functions. However, you'll find plenty of shell scripts that do not adhere to this recommendation. Most of the time, it will not cause a problem as long as you are using unique variable names throughout your script.

Exit Statuses and Return Codes

Functions are really like shell scripts within a shell script. Just like a shell script, a function has an exit status, sometimes called a return code. This exit status can be explicitly set by using the **return** statement and following it with the status you would like to return. If no **return** statement is used, then the exit status of the function is the exit status of the last command executed in the function.

The **return** statement only accepts a number. Only integers between 0 and 255 can be used as an exit status. An exit status of 0 signifies the successful completion of a command or function. A non-zero exit status indicates some type of error. To access the exit status of a function, use **$?** immediately after the function is called.

In this snippet, the value of **$?** will be the exit status of **the my_function** function.

```
my_function
echo $?
```

You can use the exit status of a function to make a decision. For example, you can check to see if the exit status is 0. If it is not, then you know some sort of error occurred. At that point you could do some sort of error handling, for example.

Before we wrap up this chapter, I want to show you an example of a function that you might actually use in one of your scripts. The **backup_file** function will create a backup of a file and place it into the **/var/tmp** directory. I use this kind of function when my script modifies several files and I want to make sure I have a copy to view or restore, just in case something unexpected happens.

In any case, the first line of the function checks to see whether what was passed in is a file and if it exists. If it is a file and it does exist, a variable called **BACKUP_FILE** is created. It starts off with **/var/tmp**, followed by the basename of the passed in file, the current date, and the PID of the shell script.

The **basename** command removes any leading directory components and returns just the file name. The **basename** of **/etc/hosts** is just **hosts**. The **date** command is using a nice format of the year, followed by the month, and finally the day, all separated by dashes. The special variable **$$** represents the PID of the currently running shell script. I use this so if I run the script multiple times on the same day, the PID will be different each time and thus the existing backups will not be overwritten.

In this snippet, the **backup_file** function is called with **/etc/hosts** as a parameter. This will create a copy of that file and place it in the temp directory as just described. Finally, there is an **if** statement that examines the return code of the **backup_file** function.

```
function backup_file () {
  if [ -f "$1" ]
  then
    local BACKUP_FILE="/var/tmp/$(basename
${1}).$(date +%F).$$"
    echo "Backing up $1 to ${BACKUP_FILE}"
    cp $1 $BACKUP_FILE
  fi
}

backup_file /etc/hosts
```

```
if [ $? -eq 0 ]
then
  echo "Backup succeeded!"
fi
```

We can take this example and improve it. One thing we can do is change the **if** statement to an **if/else** statement. If the file exists, let the exit status of the function be the exit status of the **cp** command. If the **cp** command returns a non-zero code, then our function has also failed. If we know for a fact that the file does not exist, we can use the **else** clause to explicitly return a non-zero exit status back to our main script.

We can also improve what happens after the function is called. If we know the function—and thus the backup—has failed, we can exit the script with a non-zero exit status. We could also do some other sort of error handling. Maybe you don't want to exit the script, but instead keep track of all the files that failed to backup. You could potentially move this bit of code into the **backup_file** function if you wanted to as well.

```
#!/bin/bash

function backup_file () {
  # This function creates a backup of a file.

  # Make sure the file exists.
  if [ -f "$1" ]
  then
    # Make the BACKUP_FILE variable.
    local BACKUP_FILE="/tmp/$(basename ${1}).$(date
+%F).$$"
    echo "Backing up $1 to ${BACKUP_FILE}"

    # The exit status of the function will be the
    # exit status of the cp command.
    cp $1 $BACKUP_FILE
  else
    # The file does not exist, so return
    # a non-zero exit status.
```

```
      return 1
   fi
}

# Call the function
backup_file /etc/hosts

# Make a decision based on the exit status.
# Note this is for demonstration purposes.
# You could have put this functionality inside the
# backup_file function.
if [ $? -eq "0" ]
then
   echo "Backup succeeded!"
else
   echo "Backup failed!"
   # Abort the script and return a non-zero status.
   exit 1
fi
```

Summary

In this chapter, we discussed the concept of DRY, which stands for Don't Repeat Yourself. If you find yourself writing the same bit of code in multiple places in your script, it's a good sign that you should use a function.

You learned that, by default, all variables are global. You learned how to use the **local** keyword to define local variables that are only available within the function that they are defined.

You also learned how to use positional parameters within your functions.

Finally, we covered how to use exit statuses with your functions.

Practice Exercises

Exercise 1:

Write a shell script that consists of a function that displays the number of files in the present working directory. Name this function "file_count" and call it in your script. If you use a variable in your function, remember to make it a local variable.

Hint: The **wc** utility is used to count the number of lines, words, and bytes.

Exercise 2:

Modify the script from the previous exercise. Make the "file_count" function accept a directory as an argument. Next, have the function display the name of the directory followed by a colon. Finally, display the number of files to the screen on the next line. Call the function three times. First on the "/etc" directory, next on the "/var" directory and finally on the "/usr/bin" directory.

Example output:

```
/etc:
    85
```

Solutions to the Practice Exercises

Exercise 1:

```
#!/bin/bash

function file_count() {
    local NUMBER_OF_FILES=$(ls | wc -l)
    echo "$NUMBER_OF_FILES"
}

file_count
```

Exercise 2:

```
#!/bin/bash

function file_count() {
    local DIR=$1
    local NUMBER_OF_FILES=$(ls $DIR | wc -l)
    echo "${DIR}:"
    echo "$NUMBER_OF_FILES"
}

file_count /etc
file_count /var
file_count /usr/bin
```

WILDCARDS

In this chapter, you will learn what wildcards are, when you can use them on the command line, the various types of wildcards, and how to incorporate them into your shell scripts.

A wildcard is a character or a string that is used to match file and directory names. You can use wildcards to create search patterns that, when expanded, will return a list of matching files and directories. Sometimes wildcards are referred to as "globs" or "glob patterns". Globbing is the act of expanding a wildcard pattern into the list of matching files and directories.

Wildcards can be used in conjunction with most Linux commands. If a command accepts a file or directory as an argument, you can use a wildcard in the argument to specify a file or set of files. You'll find yourself using wildcards with commands such as ls, rm, cp, mv, and others.

The two main wildcards are the asterisk (*****) and the question mark (**?**). The asterisk, or star as I like to call it, matches zero or more characters. It matches anything. By itself, it's not really that useful, but when you combine it with other parts of the file or directory names that you're looking for, it becomes powerful.

For example, you could use ***.txt** to find all the files that end in .txt. If you wanted to list all the files that start with the letter "a", use **a***. If you want to find all the files that start with an "a" and end in ".txt", use **a*.txt**.

The question mark matches exactly one character. If you want to find all the files that have only one character preceding ".txt", use **?.txt**. To match all the two letter files that begin with an "a", use **a?**. To match all the files that start with an "a," are then followed by exactly one more character, and then ends in ".txt", use **a?.txt**.

Character Classes

You can use something called a character class to create very specific search patterns. Start with a left bracket then list one or more characters you want to match and then end with a right bracket. For example, if you want to match a one character long file name that consists of a vowel, you can use **[aeiou]**. If you want to match files that start with "ca", followed by either an "n" or a "t", followed by zero or more characters, then use **ca[nt]***. This pattern will match files named "can", "cat", "candy", and "catch."

If you want to exclude characters in a match, use an exclamation mark. For example, if you want to find all the files that do not start with a vowel, use **[!aeiou]***. "Baseball" and "cricket" match this pattern because the first character is not an "a","e", "i," "o," or a "u."

Ranges

When using character classes, you can create a range by separating two characters with a hyphen. If you want to match all the characters from "a" to "g" use **[a-g]**. If you want to match the numbers 3, 4, 5, and 6, use **[3-6]**.

Named Character Classes

Instead of creating your own ranges, you can use predefined named character classes. These named classes represent the most commonly used ranges.

[:alpha:] - Matches alphabetic (letters). This matches both lower and uppercase letters.

[:alnum:] - Matches alphanumeric characters. This character class matches alpha and digits. In other words, it matches any uppercase letters, any lowercase letters, or any decimal digits.

[:digit:] - Represents numbers in decimal, 0 to 9

[:lower:] - Matches lowercase letters

[:space:] - Matches whitespace. This means characters such as spaces, tabs, and newline characters.

[:upper:] - Matches uppercase letters

Matching Wildcard Patterns

What if you want to match one of the wildcard characters? Then you would escape that character with a backslash (\). To escape the wildcard, simply place the backslash before the wildcard character. If you want to make your life easier, don't name your files with question marks and asterisks. However, you may end up receiving a file with these characters in them, so you'll need to know how to handle them. For example, if you want to match all the files that end with a question mark, then use *\?. An example match would be a file name "d-o-n-e?".

Wildcard Demo

If you would like to watch me demonstrate wildcards on the command

44

line, visit: http://www.linuxtrainingacademy.com/wildcard-demo/

Using Wildcards in Shell Scripts

When you want to create a script that works on a group of files or directories, use wildcards. One way to use wildcards in your scripts is the same way you use them on the command line.

This script changes to the **/var/www directory** and copies all the html files into **/var/www-just-html.**

```
#!/bin/bash
cd /var/www
cp *.html /var/www-just-html
```

Let's say you want to do something for each file that matches a wildcard. In that case, you can use a **for** loop. Let's use a **for** loop to perform an action on all the html files in a directory.

The following script simply echoes to the screen the name of the file that is about to be copied, and then copies that file from the **/var/www** directory to the **/var/www-just-html** directory. Of course, you could do something more complex in this loop if you wanted.

Notice that the wildcard expression is being used where you would normally provide a list. This wildcard expression will expand to create a list of matching file and directories. In the case that the wildcard is not matched, the **for** loop is not executed. Also notice that we are explicitly changing into a directory before we use the wildcard.

```
#!/bin/bash
cd /var/www
for FILE in *.html
do
    echo "Copying $FILE"
    cp $FILE /var/www-just-html
done
```

The output of the script might look something like this:

```
Copying about.html
Copying contact.html
Copying index.html
```

Let's modify the script just slightly. Instead of changing into the **/var/www** directory, let's include that path in the wildcard expression.

```
#!/bin/bash
for FILE in /var/www/*.html
do
    echo "Copying $FILE"
    cp $FILE /var/www-just-html
done
```

The output of the script will look something like this:

```
Copying /var/www/about.html
Copying /var/www/contact.html
Copying /var/www/index.html
```

Notice how the path is included in the output.

The following example demonstrates how not to use a wildcard. In the script, all the files ending in ".html" in the current working directory will be copied. The current working directory is the directory from which you started this script. If you wanted to get the same result as the previous scripts, you would have to change into the **/var/www** directory before you executed this script.

Instead of having this dependency live outside of your shell script, you should instead explicitly change into the desired directory with the **cd** command within your shell script or include the path in the wildcard expression.

```
#!/bin/bash
for FILE in *.html
do
    echo "Copying $FILE"
    cp $FILE /var/www-just-html
done
```

Review

In this chapter, you learned how to use wildcards. You learned that the asterisk matches zero or more characters. You also learned that the question mark matches exactly one of any character. You learned about character classes and how you can match any character that is included between the brackets.

You were taught about ranges and how you can create your own custom ranges by starting with a character, following it by a hyphen, and then ending it with another character. Finally, you learned about the various named character classes and how they can be used to match common sets of characters such as digits, upper case letters, and lowercase letters.

Finally, we looked at how you can use wildcards in your shell scripts in conjunction with loops. You also learned that if you do not supply a directory in the wildcard expression or change into a directory before using the wildcard expression, the wildcard expression will operate on the contents of your current directory.

Practice Exercises

Exercise 1:

Write a shell script that renames all files in the current directory that end in ".jpg" to begin with today's date in the following format: YYYY-MM-DD. For example, if a picture of my cat was in the current directory and today was October 31, 2016 it would change name from "mycat.jpg" to "2016-10-31-mycat.jpg".

Hint: Look at the format options for the date command.

For "extra credit", make sure to gracefully handle instances where there are no ".jpg" files in the current directory. (Hint: **man bash** and read the section on the nullglob option.)

Exercise 2:

Write a script that renames files based on the file extension. The script should prompt the user for a file extension. Next, it should ask the user what prefix to prepend to the file name(s). By default, the prefix should be the current date in YYYY-MM-DD format. If the user simply presses enter, the current date will be used. Otherwise, whatever the user entered will be used as the prefix. Next, it should display the original file name and the new name of the file. Finally, it should rename the file.

Example output 1:

```
Please enter a file extension: jpg
Please enter a file prefix:  (Press ENTER for 2015-
08-10). vacation
Renaming mycat.jpg to vacation-mycat.jpg.
```

Example output 2:

```
Please enter a file extension: jpg
Please enter a file prefix:  (Press ENTER for 2015-
08-10).
Renaming mycat.jpg to 2015-08-10-mycat.jpg.
```

Solutions to the Practice Exercises

Exercise 1:

```
#!/bin/bash

# Optional:
# Uncomment the following line to avoid an error when
no jpg files are found.
# shopt -s nullglob

# YYYY-MM-DD
```

```
DATE=$(date +%F)

for FILE in *.jpg
do
  mv $FILE ${DATE}-${FILE}
done
```

Exercise 2:

```
#!/bin/bash

# YYYY-MM-DD
DATE=$(date +%F)

read -p "Please enter a file extension: " EXTENSION
read -p "Please enter a file prefix:  (Press ENTER
for ${DATE}). " PREFIX

if [ -z "$PREFIX" ]
then
  PREFIX="$DATE"
fi

for FILE in *.${EXTENSION}
do
  NEW_FILE="${PREFIX}-${FILE}"
  echo "Renaming $FILE to ${NEW_FILE}."
  mv $FILE ${NEW_FILE}
done
```

CASE STATEMENTS

You already know how to make decisions and vary the flow of your scripts by using **if** statements. If you find yourself using an **if** statement to compare the same variable against different values, you could use a case statement in its place. Some people argue that, for these situations, a case statement is easier to read.

You'll see case statement in shell scripts and you'll want to at least understand what they are doing and how they work. One common place to find case statements in use is in system startup scripts.

Here is an example **if** statement that could also be a case statement.

```
#!/bin/bash
if [ "$1" = "start" ]
then
   /usr/sbin/sshd
elif [ "$1" = "stop" ]
then
   kill $(cat /var/run/sshd.pid)
elif [ "$1" = "restart" ]
then
   kill $(cat /var/run/sshd.pid)
   /usr/sbin/sshd
elif [ "$1" = "reload" ]
```

```
then
  kill -HUP $(cat /var/run/sshd.pid)
else
  echo "Usage: $0 start|stop|restart|reload"
  exit 1
fi
```

To create a case statement, start with the word **case**, follow it with an expression (most commonly a variable), and end the line with the word **in**.

Next, list a pattern or value you want to test against the variable. End the pattern with a parenthesis. If that pattern is matched, the commands following it will be executed. The execution will stop when a double semicolon is reached and the script will continue after the case statement. You can test for multiple values using the same pattern. Finally, the case statement is ended with **esac**, which is "case" spelled backwards.

```
case "$VAR" in
    pattern_1)
        # Commands go here.
        ;;
    pattern_N)
        # Commands go here.
        ;;
esac
```

Here's an example case statement. You'll find something similar to this in startup scripts or scripts that are used to control the behavior of a program.

This case statement examines the value of **$1**. Remember that **$1** is the first argument supplied to the shell script. If **$1** is equal to "start", then **/usr/sbin/sshd** is executed. If **$1** is equal to "stop", then the **kill** command is executed. If **$1** doesn't match "start" or "stop", nothing happens and the shell script continues after the case statement.

Note that the patterns are case sensitive. If someone were to execute this shell script and use "START" in all capital letters as the first argument, nothing would happen. This case statement only matches "start" in all lowercase letters and "stop" in all lowercase letters.

```
case "$1" in
   start)
      /usr/sbin/sshd
      ;;
   stop)
      kill $(cat /var/run/sshd.pid)
      ;;
esac
```

Here is a slightly modified version of the case statement. In the following example, a wildcard is used. Wildcards are covered more in depth in another chapter in this book. What you learn about pattern matching there applies to the case statement as well.

In this example, anything other than "start" and "stop" will cause the last pattern to be matched. In that case, the **echo** and **exit** commands will be executed.

```
case "$1" in
   start)
      /usr/sbin/sshd
      ;;
   stop)
      kill $(cat /var/run/sshd.pid)
      ;;
   *)
      echo "Usage: $0 start|stop"
      exit 1
      ;;
esac
```

This is yet another slightly modified version of the same case statement. This time, you might notice that a pipe was used. You can use the pipe as an OR. So, if **$1** is equal to "start" in all lowercase letters or "START" in all uppercase letters, the **sshd** command is executed.

We did the same thing with "stop." Like the previous example, the wildcard will act as a catch-all and match anything else.

```
case "$1" in
   start|START)
      /usr/sbin/sshd
      ;;
   stop|STOP)
      kill $(cat /var/run/sshd.pid)
      ;;
   *)
      echo "Usage: $0 start|stop" ; exit 1
      ;;
esac
```

Take a look at this example:

```
read -p "Enter y or n: " ANSWER
case "$ANSWER" in
   [yY]|[yY][eE][sS])
       echo "You answered yes."
       ;;
   [nN]|[nN][oO])
       echo "You answered no."
       ;;
   *)
       echo "Invalid answer."
       ;;
esac
```

Here we are asking for input from the user. This input is stored in the variable **ANSWER**. Even though you may ask the user to enter a lowercase "y" or a lower case "n", they may do something slightly different. Instead of being so strict, you can adjust the pattern matching in your case statement.

Like I said earlier, all the rules for wildcards are in play for the pattern matching section of the case statement. Here we are going to use character classes.

A quick reminder, a character class is simply a list of characters between brackets. A character class matches exactly one character and a match occurs for any of the characters included between the brackets.

The first character class in this is example is lowercase "y" and upper case "y." **[yY]** If the user enters a lower case or an uppercase "y", the first pattern will match and then "You answered yes" will be echoed to the screen. Also, if the user entered "yes", using any combination of upper or lowercase letters, the pattern following the pipe will match and "You answered yes" will be echoed to the screen. That pattern is 3 characters in length using 3 character classes. **[yY][eE][sS]** The first character class is a lowercase and uppercase "y", the second is a lowercase and uppercase "e", and the third is a lowercase and uppercase "s." We use the exact same concept to match for the "n" or "no" answer.

The last pattern is an asterisk, so it will match anything that did not match the above patterns.

You don't have to use the star wildcard by itself. In the following example, the first pattern will match anything that starts with a lowercase or uppercase "y". This will include "y", "yes", or even "yup."

```
read -p "Enter y or n: " ANSWER
case "$ANSWER" in
    [yY]*)
        echo "You answered yes."
        ;;
    *)
        echo "You answered something else."
        ;;
esac
```

Review

In this chapter, you learned what case statements are used for and how to create them. If you find yourself using an **if** statement to compare the same variable against different values, you can use a case statement in its place.

You learned how to create patterns using wildcards. You also learned how to execute the same block of code for multiple values by separating the patterns with a pipe.

Practice Exercises

Exercise 1:

Create a startup script for an application called sleep-walking-server, which is provided below. The script should be named sleep-walking and accept "start" and "stop" as arguments. If anything other than "start" or "stop" is provided as an argument, display a usage statement: "Usage sleep-walking start|stop" and terminate the script with an exit status of 1.

To start sleep-walking-server, use this command: **"/tmp/sleep-walking-server &"**

To stop sleep-walking-server, use this command: **"kill $(cat /tmp/sleep-walking-server.pid)"**

Here are the contents of "sleep-walking-server". Be sure to put this file in **/tmp** and run **chmod 755 /tmp/sleep-walking-server** so that it is executable.

```
#!/bin/bash

# Instructions:
#   Place this script in /tmp
#
# Description:
```

```
#    This script simulates a service or a daemon.

PID_FILE="/tmp/sleep-walking-server.pid"
trap "rm $PID_FILE; exit" SIGHUP SIGINT SIGTERM
echo "$$" > $PID_FILE

while true
do
    :
done
```

Solutions to the Practice Exercises

Exercise 1:

```
#!/bin/bash

# This is a startup script for sleep-walking-server
#
# Be sure to copy the sleep-walking-server file
# into /tmp and "chmod 755 /tmpsleep-walking-server"

case "$1" in
  start)
    /tmp/sleep-walking-server &
    ;;
  stop)
    kill $(cat /tmp/sleep-walking-server.pid)
    ;;
  *)
    echo "Usage: $0 start|stop"
    exit 1
esac
```

LOGGING

In this chapter, you will learn why you may want to using logging in your shell scripts. You'll also learn about the syslog standard and how to generate messages that conform to that standard. Finally, you'll learn how to create your very own custom logging functions

If you want to keep a record of what occurred during the execution of a shell script, you'll want to employ some sort of logging mechanism. Logs can store any type of information you want, but they typically answer who, what, when, where, and why something occurred.

Logs can be useful when your shell script performs several actions or produces a lot of output that might scroll off your screen. Also, if you plan to run your script unattended via cron or some other means, you might want a way to look back and see exactly what happened and when it happened during a previous run.

The Linux operating system uses the syslog standard for message logging. This allows programs and applications to generate messages that can be captured, processed, and stored by the system logger. It eliminates the need for each and every application having to implement a logging mechanism. That means we can take advantage of this logging system in our shell scripts.

Before we start using it, let's briefly talk about how it works. The syslog standard uses facilities and severities to categorize messages. Each message is labeled with a facility code and a severity level. The various combinations of facilities and severities can be used to determine how a message is handled.

Facilities are used to indicate what type of program or what part of the system the message originated from. For example, messages that are labeled with the **kern** facility originate from the Linux kernel. Messages that are labeled with the **mail** facility come from applications involved in handling mail.

There are several facilities. If your script is involved in handling mail, you could use the **mail** facility for logging. If it's not clear what facility to use, you can simply use the **user** facility. Also, the facilities ranging from local0 to local7 are to be used to create custom logs. These facilities would also be appropriate for custom written shell scripts.

Each facility has a number and a keyword associated with it. This table lists the syslog facilities.

```
Number Keyword  Description
0      kern     kernel messages
1      user     user-level messages
2      mail     mail system
3      daemon   system daemons
4      auth     security/authorization messages
5      syslog   messages generated by syslogd
6      lpr      line printer subsystem
7      news     network news subsystem
8      uucp     UUCP subsystem
9      clock    daemon
10     authpriv security/authorization messages
11     ftp      FTP daemon
12     -        NTP subsystem
13     -        log audit
```

```
14        -          log alert
15        cron       clock daemon
16        local0     local use 0 (local0)
17        local1     local use 1 (local1)
18        local2     local use 2 (local2)
19        local3     local use 3 (local3)
20        local4     local use 4 (local4)
21        local5     local use 5 (local5)
22        local6     local use 6 (local6)
23        local7     local use 7 (local7)
```

The severities are emergency, alert, critical, error, warning, notice, info, and debug. The most severe message is an emergency message and the least severe message is a debugging message.

This table lists each of the severities including their code, keyword, and description.

Code	Severity	Keyword	Description
0	Emergency	emerg (panic)	System is unusable
1	Alert	alert	Action must be taken immediately
2	Critical	crit	Critical conditions
3	Error	err (error)	Error conditions
4	Warning	warning (warn)	Warning conditions
5	Notice	notice	Normal but significant condition
6	Info	info	Informational messages
7	Debug	debug	Debug-level messages

These combinations of facilities and severities are used by the system logger to handle these messages. Most messages are simply written to a file. Each distribution uses a slightly different set of defaults, and these logging rules are configurable and can be changed. You'll find many messages stored in **/var/log/messages** on some distributions while others use **/var/log/syslog**, for example. You'll have to consult the documentation for the system logger that is in use for the system. It's typically one of syslogd, rsyslog, or syslog-ng, although there are several other possibilities.

The `logger` Utility

Now that you know about the standard logging system that is in play, you can take advantage of this in your shell scripts by using the **logger** command.

The logger command generates syslog messages. In its simplest form you simply supply a message to the **logger** utility. By default, the **logger** utility creates messages using the user facility and the notice severity.

```
logger "Message"
```

If you want to specify the severity, use the **-p** option followed by the facility, then a period, and then the severity. For example, to use the **local0** facility and the **info** severity, you would run **logger -p local0.info** and follow that with the message.

```
logger -p local0.info "Message"
```

If you want to tag your message, use the **-t** option. Typically, you'll want to use the name of your script as the tag. This way, you can search for the name of your script in a log file to extract just the messages for your script.

```
logger -t myscript -p local0.info "Message"
```

If you want to include the PID, or process ID, in the log message, use the **-i** option.

```
logger -i -t myscript "Message"
```

Let's look at the messages generated by the following **logger** commands.

The first **logger** command is used without any options. You can see that it generates a message with a time stamp and includes the message passed to the **logger** command. This message will be routed based on the system logger configuration. For most distributions, this message will end up in the **/var/log/messages** file or the **/var/log/syslog** file.

```
$ logger "Message"
Aug  2 01:22:34 linuxsvr jason: Message
```

The next **logger** command generates the same message, but this time we have specified the facility and severity. Remember that different facilities and severities can cause the system logger to route the messages to a different log file.

```
$ logger -p local0.info "Message"
Aug  2 01:22:41 linuxsvr jason: Message
```

If you want to display the message to the screen in addition to sending it to the logging system, use the "-s" option.

```
$ logger -s -p local0.info "Message"
jason: Message   # <-- Displayed on screen.
```

This **logger** command makes use of a tag. The message that it generates now contains the specified tag.

```
$ logger -t myscript -p local0.info "Message"
Aug  2 01:22:44 linuxsvr myscript: Message
```

The next **logger** command uses the **-i** option which causes the PID to be included in brackets in the log message. If multiple copies of your script can run at the same time, having a PID can help differentiate the logs being generated by one instance of the script vs logs generated by another instance of the script.

```
$ logger -i -t myscript "Message"
Aug  2 01:22:53 linuxsvr myscript[12986]: Message
```

You can even create a function in your shell script to handle logging. Here is an example from one of my scripts.

```
logit () {
  local LOG_LEVEL=$1
  shift
```

```
  MSG=$@
  TIMESTAMP=$(date +"%Y-%m-%d %T")
  if [ $LOG_LEVEL = 'ERROR' ] || $VERBOSE
  then
    echo "${TIMESTAMP} ${HOST}
${PROGRAM_NAME}[${PID}]: ${LOG_LEVEL} ${MSG}"
  fi
}
```

This function, named **logit**, expects that a log level be passed into it followed by a message. It assigns the first thing passed into it to the **LOG_LEVEL** variable. Next, **shift** is run to shift the positional parameters to the left. These means that the special variable **$@** contains everything except the first positional parameter which we already used for our **LOG_LEVEL** variable. Everything that is left over is assigned to the **MSG** variable. Next, a **TIMESTAMP** variable is created and assigned some output from the date command.

If the **LOG_LEVEL** is "ERROR" or the **VERBOSE** global variable is set to **true**, a message is echoed to the screen which includes information such as the timestamp, log level, and the message.

Instead of using **echo**, this function could employ the use of the **logger** command, if we wanted to do that.

Here are some examples of calling this function. The first time it is called, the **INFO** log level is used and the message is "Processing data." If the command **fetch-data $HOST** fails, then the **logit** function is called with an **ERROR** log level and a message that states "Could not fetch data from $HOST."

The **fetch-data** command in this example is made up. It could be another script, for example. In any case, this gives you an idea of how you can use a custom written logging function.

```
logit INFO "Processing data."

fetch-data $HOST || logit ERROR "Could not fetch data
```

```
from $HOST"
```

Review

In this chapter, you learned why you may want to use logging in your shell scripts. You also learned about the syslog standard and how to generate messages with the **logger** utility that take advantage of this standard. Finally, you learned how to create and use your very own custom logging functions.

Practice Exercises

Exercise 1:

Write a shell script that displays one random number on the screen and also generates a syslog message with that random number. Use the "user" facility and the "info" facility for your messages.

Hint: Use $RANDOM

Exercise 2:

Modify the previous script so that it uses a logging function. Additionally, tag each syslog message with "randomly" and include the process ID. Generate 3 random numbers.

Solutions to the Practice Exercises

Exercise 1:

```
#!/bin/bash

MESSAGE="Random number: $RANDOM"

echo "$MESSAGE"
logger -p user.info "$MESSAGE"
```

Exercise 2:

```
#!/bin/bash

function my_logger() {
  local MESSAGE=$@
  echo "$MESSAGE"
  logger -i -t randomly -p user.info "$MESSAGE"
}

my_logger "Random number: $RANDOM"
my_logger "Random number: $RANDOM"
my_logger "Random number: $RANDOM"
```

DEBUGGING

In this chapter, you will learn about the options built into bash that will help you find and fix errors in your shell scripts. You will also learn how to use variables to control the behavior of your shell scripts. We'll also talk about syntax highlighting and how that can help you avoid common mistakes. You'll learn about a special bash variable that you can use to get valuable information about what is happening inside of your scripts. Finally, you'll learn about the differences between Windows and Linux file types and the problems you may encounter if you plan to use multiple operating systems to create scripts.

A software bug is an error in a computer program that causes it to produce an unexpected or incorrect result. Most bugs are really mistakes in the program's code or in its design. If you encounter a bug or an error in one of your scripts, you'll want to see exactly what is happening during the execution of that script.

Maybe something isn't working as you initially anticipated and you want to figure out where things are going wrong and how you can update your script so that it performs as expected. Sometimes your script will produce an incorrect result or behave in unintended ways. Sometimes it will simply stop because of a syntax error or typo. This process of finding errors in your script or fixing unexpected behaviors is called debugging.

The bash shell provides some options that can help you in debugging your scripts. You can use these options by updating the first line in your script to include one or more of these options. The most popular of these options is the **-x** option.

The **-x** option prints commands and their arguments as they are executed. This means that, instead of variables being displayed, the values of those values are displayed. The same thing goes for expansions. Wildcards aren't displayed, but what they expand to is displayed. You'll sometimes hear this type of debugging called "print debugging," "tracing," or an "x-trace."

If you are using this option in a shell script, simply add **-x** to the end of the shebang line.

```
#!/bin/bash -x
```
If you want to do this at the command line, run **set -x**. Use **set +x** to stop this debugging behavior. You can also use this option for just a portion of your script. Just before you want to start displaying the commands to the screen, add a **set -x** line. Place **set +x** on a line after the section of the shell script that you're debugging.

Here is a very simple example that demonstrates the use of the **-x** option. You can see that **-x** has been added to the end of the shebang.

```
#!/bin/bash -x
TEST_VAR="test"
echo "$TEST_VAR"
```
Output:

```
+ TEST_VAR=test
+ echo test
test
```

You'll notice that there are lines that start with a plus sign. Those are the commands that are being executed from the script. In this example, there are two commands that are executed. The first is setting the value of the **TEST_VAR** variable. The second command is to **echo** that value to the screen. In the output, the result of the **echo** command, which is "test," is displayed. There is no plus sign in front of it because it is output as a result of a command and not a command itself.

Here is another example. This one shows how you can turn debugging on for just a portion of your script. First, the **TEST_VAR** variable is set. You'll see in the output that nothing is listed for this command because debugging isn't on at this point. The next line turns on debugging with the **set -x** command. Again, nothing is displayed in the output for this action. Now the **TEST_VAR** is echoed to the screen. The **echo** command is displayed because debugging is now own. Of course, the output of the echo command is displayed next on the screen. We use the **set +x** command to turn off debugging. That set command is displayed on the screen. Finally, the hostname command is executed and only its output is displayed.

Again, this is to demonstrate how you can encapsulate a block of code with **set -x** and **set +x** to debug that particular section of code. You can do the exact same thing with the other options that we'll be covering next.

```
#!/bin/bash
TEST_VAR="test"
set -x
echo $TEST_VAR
set +x
hostname


+ echo test
test
+ set +x
```

```
linuxsvr
```

Another useful option that can help you find errors in your scripts is the **-e** option. It causes your script to exit immediately if a command exits with a non-zero status. Remember that an exit status of zero indicates the successful completion of a command and any exit status other than zero indicates some type of error. This can really help you pin-point exactly where the problem is. You can use this in combination with other options including the **-x** option.

When used as an argument to the bash command, these options act like any other options for other commands. Options that do not take arguments can be combined and only one hyphen is required followed by the options. Also, it doesn't matter which order they are used. You can use **-ex** or **-xe**. If you want, you can use a hyphen before each option, but this is unconventional.

These four examples are equivalent in functionality.

```
#!/bin/bash -ex
```

```
#!/bin/bash -xe
```

```
#!/bin/bash -e -x
```

```
#!/bin/bash -x -e
```

Here is an example using the **-e** option. First, a value is assigned to the variable **FILE_NAME**. Next the **ls** command is executed using **FILE_NAME** as an argument. Finally, the contents of the **FILE_NAME** variable are displayed on the screen. However, when you execute this script, the **ls** command returns a non-zero exit status since the file does not exist. Because the **-e** option was used, the execution of the program halts and the echo command is never attempted.

```
#!/bin/bash -e
FILE_NAME="/not/here"
ls $FILE_NAME
echo $FILE_NAME
```

Output:

```
ls: cannot access /not/here: No such file or
directory
```

This time we'll use both the -e and -x options. The -x option causes the commands to be displayed to the screen. First, it displays the creation of the **FILE_NAME** variable. Next, it displays the **ls** command. You can clearly see what **ls** is doing in this example. It is trying to display information about a file named **/not/here**. Of course, this causes an error and the script stops because of the **-e** option.

```
#!/bin/bash -ex
FILE_NAME="/not/here"
ls $FILE_NAME
echo $FILE_NAME
```

Output:

```
+ FILE_NAME=/not/here
+ ls /not/here
ls: cannot access /not/here: No such file or
directory
```

Yet another useful option that can help you in the debugging process is the **-v** option. It prints the shell commands just like they are read from the script. It prints everything before any substitutions and expansions are applied. The **-x** option performs variable and wildcard expansion, but the **-v** option does not. You can use them in combination to see what a line looks like before and after substitutions and expansions occur.

Here is an example of the **-v** option. It causes every line of the script to be displayed on the screen before it is executed. You'll notice that the lines are exactly as they are in the shell script. In this script, the only thing that happens is that "test" gets echoed to the screen.

```
#!/bin/bash -v
TEST_VAR="test"
echo "$TEST_VAR"
```

Output:

```
#!/bin/bash -v
TEST_VAR="test"
echo "$TEST_VAR"
test
```

Here is what would happen if we added the **-x** option to the previous script. What's useful about this output is that we can see the how a command looks in the shell script and how it actually gets executed. Take the **echo** command, for example. We can see that, in the script, we run **echo $TEST_VAR** and that actually causes **echo test** to be executed.

```
#!/bin/bash -vx
TEST_VAR="test"
+ TEST_VAR=test
echo "$TEST_VAR"
+ echo test
test
```

From the command line, using a bash shell, you can run **help set**. That will display information about the options we covered in this lesson plus the other options that are available. You might want to pipe this output to a pager like **less** so you can easily scroll through all the options and their descriptions.

```
$ help set | less
set: set [-abefhkmnptuvxBCHP] [-o option-name] [--]
[arg ...]
    Set or unset values of shell options and
positional parameters.

    Change the value of shell attributes and
positional parameters, or
    display the names and values of shell variables.

    Options:
      -a  Mark variables which are modified or
created for export.
      -b  Notify of job termination immediately.
      -e  Exit immediately if a command exits with a
non-zero status.
#### Output truncated #####
```

Many times, using **-x**, **-e**, and **-v** is sufficient, but if you want a bit more control over debugging, you can create your own code to do it. One method I personally use is to create a variable called **DEBUG**. I set this to **true** if I'm currently debugging or **false** if I'm not. I'm taking advantage of the bash built-in Booleans of **true** and **false**.

If you want to use a Boolean, do not quote them. If you were to quote "**true**", for example, then it will act as a string. That's fine, but then you'll have to do string comparisons. Using Booleans simplifies testing for the **DEBUG** condition in your script.

Here is a simple example of using a **DEBUG** variable with a Boolean value. You can test if **DEBUG** is set to **true** by using an **if** statement. Since **DEBUG** is **true**, the **if** statement is true and **echo "Debug mode ON"** is executed. If you were to set **DEBUG=false**, the **if** statement would be **false** and the **else** block would be executed.

```
#!/bin/bash
DEBUG=true
if $DEBUG
then
  echo "Debug mode ON."
else
  echo "Debug mode OFF."
fi
```

You can use a DEBUG variable in conjunction with ANDS or ORs. Remember that the double ampersand means AND. It will only allow commands to be executed after it if the return code of the preceding command was 0. The **true** Boolean always returns a zero exit status.

In this first example, **DEBUG** is set to **true**. Since that is a zero exit status, the **echo "Debug mode ON."** command is executed.

```
#!/bin/bash
DEBUG=true
$DEBUG && echo "Debug mode ON."
```

You can use this pattern to execute certain commands when **DEBUG** is set to **true**. The double pipe symbol represents OR. If the command preceding an OR returns a non-zero exit status, then the command following the OR will be executed. The **false** Boolean always returns a non-zero exit status. In the following example, **DEBUG** is set to **false**. Since that is a non-zero exit status, the echo **"Debug mode OFF."** command is executed.

```
#!/bin/bash
DEBUG=false
$DEBUG || echo "Debug mode OFF."
```

You can use the following type of pattern to skip the execution of certain commands when **DEBUG** is set to **true**. If **DEBUG** succeeds, then what follows the OR will not be executed. This can prove useful when you are in the process of writing a script. You may not want or need to execute some commands that will repeat work already performed or take a long time to run, for example. This can speed up the creation of your new scripts, so, it's good for debugging and writing scripts.

```
#!/bin/bash
DEBUG=true
$DEBUG || echo "Debug mode OFF."
```

Another thing you can do is to set the value of the **DEBUG** variable to **echo**. Next, place **$DEBUG** before each line in your script. If **DEBUG** is set to **echo**, then whatever would normally have been executed is simply echoed to the screen.

In this example, the output to the screen is simply **ls** because what gets executed is **echo ls**.

```
#!/bin/bash
DEBUG="echo"
$DEBUG ls
```

Output:

```
ls
```

Here is an example where the **DEBUG** line has been commented out. This causes the value of **DEBUG** to be to nothing. That leaves the remainder of the line, which is a space followed by **ls**. That means the **ls** command will execute. Again, this is another simple way to turn debugging on and off in your scripts.

```
#!/bin/bash
#DEBUG="echo"
```

```
$DEBUG ls
```

Output:

```
solution-01.sh solution-02.sh
```

You can even create your own debug function and add whatever you would like around each command, or choose NOT to execute the command if you wish. Use the special variable **$@** inside your function to access everything passed to the function.

In this example, the command that will be executed is simply echoed to the screen before being executed. You could, of course, do something more complicated and useful. Maybe you could write this information to a log file and include time stamps showing exactly when each command was executed.

```
#!/bin/bash

debug() {
  echo "Executing: $@"
  $@
}
```

Manual Copy and Paste

Sometimes I open a second terminal window and go through the shell script one line at a time. I will copy and paste the first line, then the second, one at a time on the command line until I find where the problem is. Remember that you can use this in conjunction with **set -x** or any other option you think will help you.

Syntax Highlighting

Many times, bugs or errors in a shell script are due to a simple syntax error. Maybe you mistyped something or forgot to include a closing bracket, for example. These simple mistakes can be caught before you even try to execute your script if you are using an editor with syntax highlighting.

Two of the most commonly used editors on a Linux system are vim and emacs. By default, they both have syntax highlighting. Here are a couple of screenshots from those editors to show you what this looks like.

```
#!/bin/bash

debug() {
   echo "Executing: $@"
   $@
}

debug ls
```

Of course, there are plenty of other editors with highlighting support. You'll have to check the documentation for your particular editor to see if shell script highlighting is supported and, if so, how to enable it.

Editors with syntax highlighting support:

- vi / vim

- emacs

- nano

- gedit

- kate

- geany

- Many others

PS4

You may be familiar with the **PS1** environment variable. It controls what is displayed as your command prompt. There are other variables similar to this one. The one that is valuable for shell script debugging is **PS4**.

PS4 is expanded and displayed before each command during an execution trace. That means, when you are using **set -x** or the **-x** option for your bash script, the contents of **PS4** are printed to the screen. By default, this is the plus sign. However, we can explicitly set the **PS4** variable. Bash includes several built-in variables such as **$BASH_SOURCE**, which is the name of the script itself, and **$LINENO**, which is the line number in the script. To see even more variables, visit: http://www.gnu.org/software/bash/manual/html_node/Bash-Variables.html

Here is an example of using the **PS4** variable. This script sets **PS4** to "+ **$BASH_SOURCE : $LINENO : ".

```
#!/bin/bash -x
PS4='+ $BASH_SOURCE : $LINENO : '
TEST_VAR="test"
echo "$TEST_VAR"
```

Output:

```
+ PS4='+ $BASH_SOURCE : $LINENO : '
+ ./test.sh : 3 : TEST_VAR=test
+ ./test.sh : 4 : echo test
test
```

You can see that when the script gets executed, the output changes after the **PS4** variable is set. This can make the output clearer. For example, if we have a problem with the **echo** command, we know we can edit the script and head straight for line 4.

Here is a more advanced example. It just includes more information, such as the function name.

```
#!/bin/bash -x
PS4='+ ${BASH_SOURCE}:${LINENO}:${FUNCNAME[0]}() '
debug() {
  echo "Executing: $@"
  $@
}
debug ls
```

Output:

```
+ PS4='+ ${BASH_SOURCE}:${LINENO}:${FUNCNAME[0]}() '
+ /tmp/j:7:() debug ls
+ /tmp/j:4:debug() echo 'Executing: ls'
Executing: ls
+ /tmp/j:5:debug() ls
```

You can see how the **PS4** variable allowed us to print the function name using the built-in variable **FUNCNAME**.

File Types

Plain text files, like we are working with for shell scripts, contain a control character to represent the end of a line. For Unix and Linux systems, the control character representing a new line is a Line Feed.

DOS or Windows systems actually use two characters to represent a new line: a carriage return and a line feed.

If you've ever created a text file on a Linux system and sent it to someone who is using a Windows system, it may very well display as one long line on their computer. This is due to the lack of carriage returns.

If you were to do the opposite, create a text file on a Windows system and open it on a Linux system, there will be additional characters, specifically carriage returns, in that file. The problem in this situation is that when you display the contents of the file to the screen, you will not see the additional carriage returns. For example, if you ran **cat script.sh** and that file had carriage returns in it, you wouldn't see them. You have to run **cat -v script.sh** to display non-printable characters, like carriage returns. Carriage returns are represented by the caret symbol followed by M (**^M**).

```
$ cat script.sh
#!/bin/bash
# This file contains carriage returns.
echo "Hello world."
$ cat -v script.sh
#!/bin/bash^M
# This file contains carriage returns.^M
echo "Hello world."^M
```

If you execute a file that contains carriage returns, you'll probably run into an error like this: **"/bin/bash^M:, No such file or directory."** The carriage return is being treated as part of the file name. In order to get this script to run, we need to remove the carriage returns.

This situation is another reason why you should always start your scripts with a shebang. If you didn't have the shebang line, the commands would be executed using your current shell. This can lead to strange things happening. The script might work as expected in some parts, but totally fail at other parts due to carriage returns. If you start getting strange errors that make no sense, check to see if there are carriage returns in your script.

In addition to using the **cat -v** command to see if there are carriage returns in a file, you can also use the **file** command. If it finds the additional carriage returns, it will alert you to the fact.

To easily remove these characters, I recommend that you use the **dos2unix** utility. It may not be installed by default on your system, so you may have to manually install it if you need it. This utility converts a DOS file—or a file with carriage returns—into a Unix file, or a file without carriage returns. There is another utility which does the opposite, and it's called **unix2dos**.

After you run the **dos2unix** command against your file, you'll find that the carriage returns are removed. You can confirm this by running the **file** command against the file. You'll notice there is no warning about CRLF line terminators.

```
$ file script.sh
script.sh: Bourne-Again shell script, ASCII text
executable, with CRLF line terminators
$ dos2unix script.sh
$ file script.sh
script.sh: Bourne-Again shell script, ASCII text
executable
```

Usually, you end up with these unwanted carriage returns in your shell scripts due to creating a file on a Windows system and uploading that file to a Linux system. If you want to create shell scripts on a Windows system, see if your editor supports Unix-style line endings. If it does support this option, turn it on. Also, some editors can convert between dos and Unix style file types.

You can also end up with unwanted characters in your shell scripts if you copy some text from your windows computer and paste it into your putty window. Even if you're using an all Linux system, the copy and paste action can get you. For example, if you copy some text from a web page that has carriage returns in it and then paste that into a text file, that file may contain those carriage returns.

Review

In this chapter, you learned how to use a few different built-in bash options to aid you in debugging shell scripts. You learned what the **-x**, **-e**, and **-v** options do and how to combine them. You also learned how to use variables to assist you in debugging and creating shell scripts. We talked about the advantages of using an editor that has syntax highlighting support. You learned about the **PS4** variable and how to use that in conjunction with an x-trace. Finally, you learned about the challenges of switching back and forth between windows and Linux, and more importantly, how to catch and correct errors caused by carriage returns.

Practice Exercises

Exercise 1:

Write a shell script that exits on error and displays commands as they will execute, including all expansions and substitutions. Use 3 **ls** commands in your script. Make the first one succeed, the second one fail, and the third one succeed. If you are using the proper options, the third **ls** command will not be executed.

Exercise 2:

Modify the previous exercise so that script continues, even if an error occurs. This time, all three **ls** commands will execute.

Solutions to the Practice Exercises

Exercise 1:

```
#!/bin/bash -ex

ls /etc/passwd
ls /move/along/nothing/to/see/here
ls /etc/passwd
```

Exercise 2:

```
#!/bin/bash -x

ls /etc/passwd
ls /move/along/nothing/to/see/here
ls /etc/passwd
```

SHELL SCRIPT CHECKLIST

1. Does your script start with a shebang?

Example:

```
#/bin/bash
```

2. Does your script include a comment describing the purpose of the script?

Example:

```
# This script creates a backup of every MySQL
database on the system.
```

3. Are the global variables declared at the top of your script, following the initial comment(s)?

Example:

```
DEBUG=true
HTML_DIR=/var/www
```

4. Have you grouped all of your functions together following the global variables?

5. Do your functions use local variables?

Example:

```
local GREETING="Hello!"
```

6. Does the main body of your shell script follow the functions?

7. Does your script exit with an explicit exit status?

Example:

```
exit 0
```

8. At the various exit points, are exit statuses explicitly used?

```
Example:
if [ ! -d "$HTML_DIR" ]
then
  echo "$HTML_DIR does not exist. Exiting."
  exit 1
fi
```

SHELL SCRIPT TEMPLATE

```
#!/bin/bash
#
# <Replace with the description and/or purpose
# of this shell script.>

GLOBAL_VAR1="one"
GLOBAL_VAR2="two"

function function_one() {
  local LOCAL_VAR1="one"
  # <Replace with function code.>
}

# Main body of the shell script starts here.
#
# <Replace with the main commands of your
# shell script.>

# Exit with an explicit exit status.
exit 0
```

The above template is comprised of a short series of best practices. First off, all scripts should start with a shebang. This is the first line of your script and it explicitly declares which interpreter is used to execute the script.

Next, you should include at least a one-line comment summarizing what the script does and why it exists. You can include more information if you like. Some people like to include information such as the original author of the script, the version of the script, and other details.

If you are going to use global variables, they should come next unless their value cannot be determined until a later point in your script.

Functions should come next. Group all of your functions together following the global variables.

Within your functions, be sure to use the **local** keyword when defining variables that are local to the function.

Following the functions section, the main portion of your shell script begins.

Finally, remember to explicitly use an exit status. If you do not supply an exit status, which is a number from 0 to 255, then the exit status of the previously executed command will be used as the exit status of your script. It's best to control this rather than leave it to chance.

At least end your script with an **exit 0** line. If your script was able to get to the last line of your script, then, in most cases, it has successfully completed. Also keep in mind the other places where your shell script may terminate. You'll want to use exit statements in those places as well. For example, if your script performs some sort of check and stops because the check failed, you'll want to exit with a non-zero exit status.

SCRIPTS FROM MY PERSONAL COLLECTION

If you would like to see some shell scripts from my personal collection, visit: https://github.com/jasonc/scripts

CONGRATULATIONS AND THANK YOU!

Congratulations for making it through this book! As a way of saying thank you for reading this book and making it to the end, I would like to give you a huge discount on my shell scripting course.

To enroll for just $15 -- 85% off the normal price of $99 -- visit:

http://www.linuxtrainingacademy.com/shell-course

I look forward to seeing you in the course!

Thanks,

Jason

OTHER BOOKS BY THE AUTHOR

Command Line Kung Fu: Bash Scripting Tricks, Linux Shell Programming Tips, and Bash One-liners
http://www.linuxtrainingacademy.com/command-line-kung-fu-book

High Availability for the LAMP Stack: Eliminate Single Points of Failure and Increase Uptime for Your Linux, Apache, MySQL, and PHP Based Web Applications
http://www.linuxtrainingacademy.com/ha-lamp-book

Linux for Beginners: An Introduction to the Linux Operating System and Command Line
http://www.linuxtrainingacademy.com/linux

Python Programming for Beginners
http://www.linuxtrainingacademy.com/python-programming-for-beginners

ADDITIONAL RESOURCES INCLUDING EXCLUSIVE DISCOUNTS FOR YOU

For even more resources, visit:
http://www.linuxtrainingacademy.com/resources

Books

Command Line Kung Fu
http://www.linuxtrainingacademy.com/command-line-kung-fu-book

Do you think you have to lock yourself in a basement reading cryptic man pages for months on end in order to have ninja-like command line skills? In reality, if you had someone share their most powerful command line tips, tricks, and patterns, you'd save yourself a lot of time and frustration. This book does just that.

High Availability for the LAMP Stack
http://www.linuxtrainingacademy.com/ha-lamp-book

Eliminate Single Points of Failure and Increase Uptime for Your Linux, Apache, MySQL, and PHP Based Web Applications

Linux for Beginners
http://www.linuxtrainingacademy.com/linux

Python Programming for Beginners
http://www.linuxtrainingacademy.com/python-programming-for-beginners

If you are interested in learning how to program, or use Python specifically, this book is for you. In it, you will learn how to install Python, which version to choose, how to prepare your computer for a great experience, and all the computer programming basics you'll need to know to start writing fully functional programs.

Courses

High Availability for the LAMP Stack
http://www.linuxtrainingacademy.com/ha-lamp-stack

Learn how to setup a highly available LAMP stack (Linux, Apache, MySQL, PHP). You'll learn about load balancing, clustering databases, creating distributed file systems, and more.

Learn Linux in 5 Days
http://www.linuxtrainingacademy.com/linux-in-5-days

Take just 45 minutes a day for the next 5 days and I will teach you exactly what you need to know about the Linux operating system. You'll learn the most important concepts and commands, and I'll even guide you step-by-step through several practical and real-world examples.

Shell Scripting
http://www.linuxtrainingacademy.com/shell-course

Cloud Hosting and VPS (Virtual Private Servers)

Digital Ocean
http://www.linuxtrainingacademy.com/digitalocean

Simple cloud hosting, built for developers. Deploy an SSD cloud server in just 55 seconds. You can have your own server for as little as $5 a month.

Web Hosting with SSH and Shell Access

Bluehost
http://www.linuxtrainingacademy.com/bluehost

99% of my websites are hosted on Bluehost. Why? Because it's incredibly easy to use with 1-click automatic WordPress installation and excellent customer service - via phone and via chat. I HIGHLY RECOMMEND using Bluehost for your first site. Also, you can use the same hosting account for multiple domains if you plan on creating more websites. Visit http://www.linuxtrainingacademy.com/bluehost to get a special discount off the regular price!

APPENDIX: TRADEMARKS

BSD/OS is a trademark of Berkeley Software Design, Inc. in the United States and other countries.

Facebook is a registered trademark of Facebook, Inc.

Firefox is a registered trademark of the Mozilla Foundation.

HP and HEWLETT-PACKARD are registered trademarks that belong to Hewlett-Packard Development Company, L.P.

IBM® is a registered trademark of International Business Machines Corp., registered in many jurisdictions worldwide.

Linux® is the registered trademark of Linus Torvalds in the U.S. and other countries.

Mac and OS X are trademarks of Apple Inc., registered in the U.S. and other countries.

Open Source is a registered certification mark of Open Source Initiative.

Sun and Oracle Solaris are trademarks or registered trademarks of Oracle Corporation and/or its affiliates in the United States and other countries.

UNIX is a registered trademark of The Open Group.

Windows is a registered trademark of Microsoft Corporation in the United States and other countries.

All other product names mentioned herein are the trademarks of their respective owners.